Mit **New Highlight Plus** · Band 1 (von 3 Bänden) bietet der Verlag Materialien zur individuellen Förderung von Schülerinnen und Schülern nach ihren jeweiligen Bedürfnissen an. Diese Materialien sind im Hinblick auf Themen, Strukturen und Vokabelstand genau auf das Schülerbuch **New Highlight** · Band 1 abgestimmt.

Die sechs Units der vorliegenden Fördermaterialien entsprechen den sechs Units von **New Highlight** · Band 1 und sind für den Einsatz nach der Behandlung der jeweiligen Schülerbuch-Unit vorgesehen. Die Aufgaben zu jeder Unit sind in drei Abschnitte eingeteilt – **Test**, **Train** und **Check** – und sollten stets in dieser Reihenfolge angeboten werden.

❚ Der Abschnitt **Test** besteht aus je sechs Aufgaben zu den Bereichen *Vocabulary*, *Communication*, *Practice* (= Grammatik), *Reading* und *Writing*, die alle in einer Sitzung gelöst werden sollten. Damit erhalten die Schülerinnen und Schüler umfassend Auskunft über den aktuellen Stand ihrer Fähigkeiten und Kenntnisse. Mit dem Ergebnis werden sie jedoch nicht allein gelassen: Am Ende jeder Testaufgabe gibt es Verweise sowohl auf die Lösung im Anhang als auch auf die Stelle im **Train**-Teil, die bei nicht ausreichender Beherrschung des jeweiligen Aspektes der Sprache (= weniger als fünf richtige Antworten) die nötigen Übungsmöglichkeiten bietet. Mit der Auswertung des **Test**-Abschnitts nehmen die Schülerinnen und Schüler die Verantwortung für die Verbesserung ihrer Englischkenntnisse selbst in die Hand.

❚ Der Abschnitt **Train** bietet eine Vielzahl verschiedener Übungen für jeden der fünf Sprachaspekte. Hier werden keine „Fallen gestellt", sondern reichlich Hilfen gegeben, damit die Schülerinnen und Schüler die besten Chancen haben, die Übungen erfolgreich zu absolvieren. Gezielte Hinweise auf „Tippzetteln" zeigen Strategien auf, die zu größerer Methodenkompetenz verhelfen. Auch zum **Train**-Abschnitt gibt es hinten im Heft Lösungen.

❚ Der Abschnitt **Check** schließlich dient den Schülerinnen und Schülern zur raschen Selbstevaluation: Nach der Bearbeitung der wiederum als Test angelegten Aufgaben können sie mithilfe von „Ampeln" ihren unmittelbaren Lernfortschritt feststellen (Lösungen hinten im Heft).

Mit **New Highlight Plus** gelangen die Schülerinnen und Schüler also von der Diagnose **(Test)** über die Übung **(Train)** zu einer verbesserten, überprüfbaren „Fitness" in Englisch **(Check)**.

Verlag und Autoren wünschen viel Erfolg!

D1619356

TEST A NEW START

1 Vocabulary

Welches Wort passt nicht in die Reihe? Streiche es durch.

1 pencil, bag, rubber, pen

2 OK, nice, great, terrible

3 you, I, we, with

4 look, listen, sign, see

5 hi, hello, happy, bye

6 September, Monday, Friday, Sunday

Lösungen: Seite 56   *Weniger als fünf richtige Antworten* ➜ *Seite 4 und 5*

2 Communication

Welche Aussagen gehören zusammen? Ziehe Linien.

1 Good morning, Mr Jones.	I'm fine, thanks.
2 Bye, Mum.	I'm not Jane. I'm Jill.
3 Hi, Jane.	Good morning, Tom.
4 Hello. How are you?	Hello, Ms Black.
5 Hello, John.	Hi. I'm Paul.
6 Hi. What's your name?	Bye, Pat.

Lösungen: Seite 56   *Weniger als fünf richtige Antworten* ➜ *Seite 6*

3 Practice

Welche Buchstaben fehlen?

1 I'_____ Tim.

2 He'_____ my teacher.

3 They'_____ nice pupils.

4 I'_____ not Sarah. I'm Emma.

5 We are_____ English. We're German.

6 They are_____ teachers. They're pupils.

Lösungen: Seite 56   *Weniger als fünf richtige Antworten* ➜ *Seite 7*

4 Reading

Lies den Text durch.

Who am I?

I'm a boy. I'm not dangerous. Sarah is late for school and I'm late too. Sarah is in year 7. I'm in Sarah's bag. A pencil case and books are in the bag too. See you tomorrow. Bye!

Nun umkreise die richtigen Wörter.

1 He's a *"boy"* / *teacher*.

2 He's *dangerous* / *nice*.

3 Sarah *is* / *isn't* late for school.

4 Sarah is in *year 8* / *year 7*.

5 He's in Sarah's *bag* / *pencil case*.

6 He's *Tom* / *Sammy*.

Lösungen: Seite 56   Weniger als fünf richtige Antworten ➜ *Seite 8*

5 Writing

Julia stellt sich vor. Ergänze die Sätze.

1 Hi. I'_____ Julia Schmidt.

2 I'm German. _____ not English.

3 I'm in _____ 5.

4 Ms Klein _____ my English teacher.

5 My English book is in my _____.

6 Now it's homework _____. Bye!

Lösungen: Seite 56   Weniger als fünf richtige Antworten ➜ *Seite 8*

1 What is it? Zeichne die angegebenen Dinge oder Personen in die Kästen.

1 This is a bus.

2 This is my bag.

3 This is my pencil case.

4 This is a girl.

5 This is a boy.

6 This is a spider.

2 Colours Schau dir die englischen Begriffe unten an. Dann ordne sie einer der folgenden Überschriften zu und markiere sie in der entsprechenden Farbe:

Personen: blau   **Gegenstände:** rot   **Tätigkeiten:** grün   **Eigenschaften:** orange

find	finish	great	Mrs Jones	mum	OK
pencil	pupil	repeat	right	sign	TV

Tipp: Zu jeder Farbe gibt es drei Begriffe.

3 Find the words. Finde im Rätsel unten die englischen Wörter für die 10 deutschen Begriffe und kringele sie ein.
Schau in zwei Richtungen: → (6 Wörter) und ↓ (4 Wörter)

1 Wort
2 Satz
3 Strophe
4 Geschichte
5 Danke.
6 Auf Wiedersehen.
7 Zeit; Uhrzeit
8 Reihenfolge
9 Jahr; Jahrgangsstufe
10 Hausaufgaben, Schularbeiten

```
S D U D B A L T I M E
T S T O R Y X H N T L
S G S R E Y E A R D S
C O I D N A L N H Y P
H O M E W O R K O T X
O D R R O G M S R T O
K B V E R S E W I A G
N Y V M D D Z O P S I
S E N T E N C E G A R
T U B I O C H O R K T
```

4 **Which word is right?** Entscheide jeweils, ob das Nomen in der Einzahl oder in der Mehrzahl stehen muss, und (umkreise) die richtigen Wörter.

1 Drake School is a great *school / schools*.

2 The *teacher / teachers* are very nice.

3 The *pupil / pupils* are nice too!

4 I'm a new *pupil / pupils*.

5 What's in my *bag / bags*?

6 A *pencil case / pencil cases*, three *book / books*, two *pencil / pencils* and a *pen / pens*.

> Tipp:
> Steht „a" vor dem Nomen, ist es die Einzahl!

5 **The missing letter** Schau dir die Wörter an und trage den fehlenden Buchstaben ein. Wenn du die eingesetzten Buchstaben von oben nach unten liest, erhältst du ein weiteres Wort aus dieser Unit.

D	A	N	G	E	__	O	U	S
	T	E	R	R	__	B	L	E
			S	I	__	N		
	T	E	A	C	__	E	R	
	P	I	C	__	U	R	E	

6 **Questions** Ergänze jeden Satz mit dem richtigen Wort aus dem Kasten.

- he
- she
- it
- we
- you
- they

1 "This is my bag." – "Is _____ new?"

2 "Tic and Tac are spiders."– "Are _____ dangerous?"

3 "This is Pam." – "Is _____ terrible?"

4 "This is Tim." – "Is _____ nice?"

5 "Hello, Tim and Pam! Are _____ at Drake School too?"

6 "We're spiders. Are _____ OK?"

1 What are they saying? Ergänze die Sätze. Der Kasten hilft dir dabei.

1 _____, Dad.

2 _____, Paul.

3 _____, boys and girls.

4 See you _____.

5 _____, Ms Hill.

→
- good morning
- hi
- tomorrow
- goodbye
- bye

2 Questions and answers Was sind die Fragen und Antworten? Schreibe sie auf.

1 name / What's / your   _____?

2 in / What year / you / are   _____?

3 you / How / are   _____?

4 – Williams / Peter / I'm   _____.

5 – year 7 / I'm / in   _____.

6 – fine / I'm / thanks   _____.

Tipp: Die Antworten 4–6 passen zu den Fragen 1–3.

3 What are they saying? Ergänze die Sätze. Der Kasten hilft dir dabei.

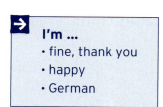

1 I'm _____.

2 _____ not _____.

3 I'm _____, _____.

→
I'm ...
- fine, thank you
- happy
- German

4 Hi! Vervollständige den Dialog.

1 Hi. _____?

2 Hi, I'm Paula. _____?

3 _____ Meg.

4 _____ year are you in?

5 _____ in year 7.

Tipp: Sieh dir S.19 im Buch an.

1 Tim and Pam Welche Satzpaare gehören zusammen?
Ziehe Linien und ergänze das fehlende Wort.

Tip: Tim and Pam
are pupils. They're
at a school in
London.

1   Tim isn't a girl.   They're _____.

2   Pam isn't a boy.   It's in _____.

3   Tim and Pam aren't teachers.   He's a _____.

4   Pam: I'm not Tim.   She's a _____.

5   Tim: You aren't dangerous, Pam.   We're _____.

6   Tim and Pam: Our school isn't in Exeter.   I'm _____.

7   Tim and Pam: We aren't German.   You're _____.

2 No! Ergänze jeden Satz mit der richtigen Form aus dem Kasten.

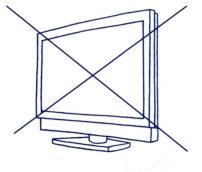

Tipp: Alle Lückensätze
drücken aus, was nicht
der Fall ist.

• 'm not
• isn't (3x)
• aren't (3x)

1   Mum: "It's homework time. It _____ TV time."

2   Pam: "My teachers are nice. They _____ terrible."

3   Tim: "Pam is in year 5. She _____ in year 6."

4   Sammy: "I'm a spider. But I _____ dangerous."

5   Teacher: "Good morning, Pam and Tim. You _____ late. Good!"

6   Pam and Tim: "We're English. We _____ German."

7   Tim: "Mr Fox is my teacher. He _____ my dad".

1 A poem Lies das Gedicht.

1 My name is Roy.
   I'm a boy.
2 My name is Herman.
   I'm not German.
3 I'm Ms Meacher.
   I'm a teacher.
4 I'm Ms Plum.
   I'm a mum.
5 I'm Mr Ladd.
   I'm a dad.
6 My name is Heide.
   And I'm a spider!

Der Dichter hat die falschen Namen benutzt. Im Kasten stehen die richtigen Namen. Aber in welche Strophen gehören sie?

1 _____

2 _____

3 _____

4 _____

5 _____

6 _____

> Tipp: Sage die Namen laut und achte auf die Aussprache. Suche dann die Strophe mit dem passenden Reim.

→
- Glad
- Gumm
- Peacher
- Ryder
- Sherman
- Troy

2 And you? Schreibe über dich.

1 _____ a _____. (Mädchen? Junge?)

2 _____. (Name?)

3 _____ a _____. (Schüler/in? Natürlich!)

4 _____ in _____. (dein Schuljahr)

5 _____. (Glücklich? Ja oder nein?)

6 _____. (Nett? Natürlich!)

> Tipp: Alle Sätze fangen mit *I'm* an.

→ **Nützliche Wörter zum Einsetzen:**
- boy/girl
- year 5
- happy/not happy
- nice

A NEW START

Wie fit bist du nun? Alles im grünen Bereich?
Mache den Check und male dabei die Ampeln entsprechend aus.

1 Vocabulary Welche Wörter passen zusammen? Ziehe Linien.

1 great   thanks

2 Mr   teacher

3 mum   goodbye

4 pupil   terrible

5 hello   dad

6 please   Ms

Lösungen: Seite 57

0–2 richtige Antworten:	rot
3–4 richtige Antworten:	gelb
5–6 richtige Antworten:	grün

2 Communication Welche Wörter sind richtig? Umkreise sie.

1 Good *morning / tomorrow*, girls and boys.

2 I'm not Paul. I'm *Paul / Peter*.

3 See you *morning / tomorrow*.

4 I'm fine, *please / thanks*.

5 *Who's / What's* your name?

6 I'm in *your / year* 7.

Lösungen: Seite 57

0–2 richtige Antworten:	rot
3–4 richtige Antworten:	gelb
5–6 richtige Antworten:	grün

3 Practice Ergänze jeden Satz mit der richtigen Form aus dem Kasten.

1 Sarah isn't German. _____ English.

2 Tom isn't a teacher. _____ a pupil.

3 Jamie and Tom aren't girls. _____ boys.

4 Jamie and Tom: "We aren't at Hill School.

_____ at Drake School."

5 Emma: "You aren't a pupil, Ms Brown.

_____ a teacher."

6 Sammy: "And _____ a spider!"

→
- He's
- I'm
- She's
- They're
- We're
- You're

Lösungen: Seite 58

0–2 richtige Antworten:	rot
3–4 richtige Antworten:	gelb
5–6 richtige Antworten:	grün

CHECK A NEW START

4 Reading Lies zuerst den Text durch.

Who is it?

He isn't a teacher.
He's a boy.
He isn't a spider.
He's at Drake School.
He's in year 8.
He's with Jill.

Tipp: Sieh dir S.14 im Schülerbuch an.

Nun umkreise die richtigen Wörter.

1 He's a *teacher / boy*.

2 *He's / He isn't* a spider.

3 He isn't at *Drake / Port* School.

4 He isn't in *year 7 / year 8*.

5 *He's / He isn't* with Jill.

6 And he's *Jack / Tom*!

Lösungen: Seite 58

0–2 richtige Antworten: rot

3–4 richtige Antworten: gelb

5–6 richtige Antworten: grün

5 Writing Saskia möchte, dass du ihr beim Internet-Chat hilfst. Schreibe die englischen Sätze.

Sie will sagen, dass …

1 sie ein Mädchen ist: I_____.

2 sie Saskia heißt: I_____.

3 Deutsche ist: I_____.

4 Schülerin ist: I_____.

5 sie in die Klasse 5 geht: I_____.

6 es Zeit für Hausaufgaben ist: It's _____.

Lösungen: Seite 58

0–2 richtige Antworten: rot

3–4 richtige Antworten: gelb

5–6 richtige Antworten: grün

© 2007 Cornelsen Verlag Berlin. Alle Rechte vorbehalten.

1 Vocabulary

Welches Wort passt nicht in die Reihe? Streiche es durch.

1 home, house, page, flat

2 bed, chair, table, garden

3 mum, room, brother, sister

4 group, kitchen, living room, bedroom

5 big, brown, blue, red

6 old, dirty, wrong, share

Lösungen: Seite 58   Weniger als fünf richtige Antworten ➜ Seite 13 und 14

2 Communication

Welche Antwort passt zu welcher Frage? Ziehe Linien.

1 Do you have a sister?   I'm 11.

2 What colour is your room?   A big TV.

3 Do you have your own room?   It's yellow and red.

4 What's your name?   No, I don't. I share a room with Sally.

5 How old are you?   Yes, I do – Sally.

6 What's in your room?   I'm Pat.

Lösungen: Seite 58   Weniger als fünf richtige Antworten ➜ Seite 15

3 Practice

Welches Wort ist richtig? Umkreise die richtigen Wörter.

1 I *have / has* a sister.

2 We *has / have* a house.

3 The boys *has / have* a nice room.

4 I *don't / doesn't* have a pet.

5 My sister *don't / doesn't* have a nice room.

6 You *don't / doesn't* have a small flat.

Lösungen: Seite 58   Weniger als fünf richtige Antworten ➜ Seite 16

4 Reading

Lies den Text durch.

The Wilsons and the new house

The house is new. It isn't old. It's very big. The garden is nice. But the kitchen is small. The bathroom is black. Terrible! The Wilsons have a nice house. But they have lots of work in the bathroom!

Yes oder No?
Setze ein ✔ in das richtige Kästchen.

		Yes.	No.
1	The house is old.	☐	☐
2	It's very small.	☐	☐
3	The garden is terrible.	☐	☐
4	The kitchen is black.	☐	☐
5	The Wilsons have a nice house.	☐	☐
6	The Wilsons have lots of work in the bathroom.	☐	☐

Lösungen: Seite 58   Weniger als fünf richtige Antworten ➔ Seite 17

5 Writing

Fabian schreibt eine E-Mail an einen englischen Schüler.
Ergänze die Sätze.

1 _____ two sisters.

2 _____ in Freiburg.

3 _____ year 5.

4 _____ Goetheschule.

5 _____ is your room? Is it white?

6 _____ a TV in your room?

Lösungen: Seite 58   Weniger als fünf richtige Antworten ➔ Seite 17

1 **My family** Finde die Wörter für die abgebildeten Familienmitglieder im Rätsel und kringele sie ein. Dann trage die Wörter unten rechts an der richtigen Stelle (1–6) ein. Übertrage nun die markierten Buchstaben unten links in die Sprechblase und du erhältst das Lösungswort.

→ 5 Wörter
↓ 1 Wort

5

```
S  D  A  D  E  A  L  I  C  H
T  O  I  S  T  G  X  L  I  T
S  I  S  T  E  R  P  F  Y  D
C  H  I  S  W  A  L  K  H  Y
U  Z  T  R  A  N  F  W  O  T
S  G  R  A  N  D  M  A  R  T
K  F  U  P  L  A  S  T  N  A
N  M  U  M  B  D  Z  O  P  S
F  R  U  G  E  N  M  E  G  A
R  O  B  R  O  T  H  E  R  T
```

6   1

3

4

2

Hi, I'm Anna.

This is my family.

I'm 10.

I'm _____ .

1 _____
2 _____
3 _____
4 _____
5 _____
6 _____

2 **Colours** Wo hört das eine Farbwort auf? Wo fängt das nächste an? Ziehe Striche. Und wo gehören die fehlenden Buchstaben hin? Füge sie ein.

3 Buchstaben: 1 Wort,
4 Buchstaben: 2 Wörter,
5 Buchstaben: 3 Wörter,
6 Buchstaben: 1 Wort

3 **Our house** Trage die gesuchten Wörter unten ein.
Daraus ergibt sich das Lösungswort (L).

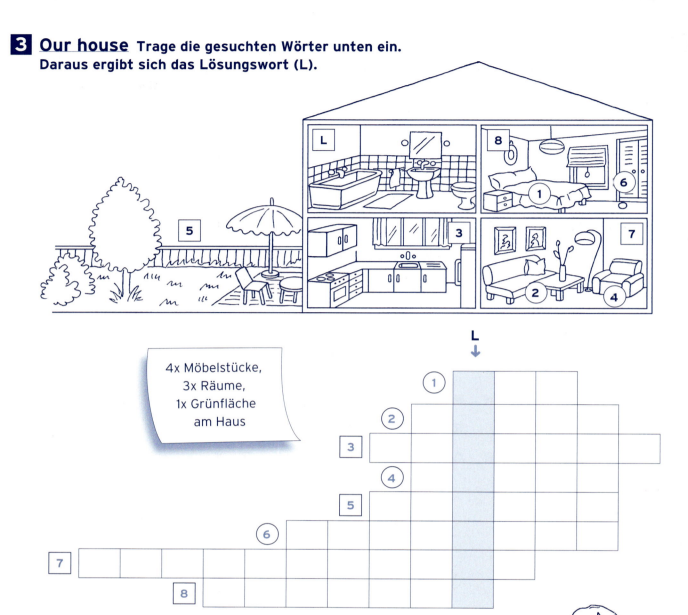

4x Möbelstücke,
3x Räume,
1x Grünfläche
am Haus

4 **This is Jack.** Ergänze jeden Satz mit dem richtigen Verb aus dem
Kasten. Schreibe den gesuchten Lösungsbuchstaben hinter die Zeile.

→
- collect
- have
- live
- pick
- share

1 Hi, I'm Jack. I _____ in a house in Exeter. (1. Buchstabe: ___)

2 I _____ a brother, Nick. (4. Buchstabe: ___)

3 I _____ a room with Nick. (1. Buchstabe: ___)

4 I _____ spiders! (3. Buchstabe: ___)

5 I _____ very small spiders. (1. Buchstabe: ___)

**Trage jetzt die Lösungsbuchstaben an der richtigen Stelle ein,
und du erhältst ein weiteres Verb:**

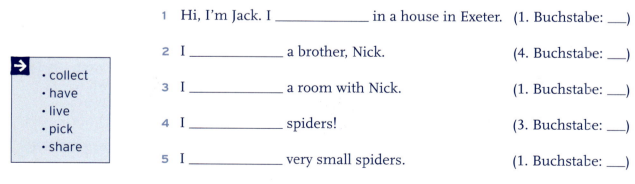

___ ___ ___ ___ ___
3   5   2   1   4

1 Do you have ... ? Dein Freund kann kein Englisch.
Stelle die Fragen für ihn.

Frage die neue Schülerin, ob sie ...

1 ein eigenes Zimmer hat: _____?

2 einen Fernseher im Zimmer hat: _____?

3 Geschwister hat: _____?

4 eine beste Freundin hat: _____?

2 Questions Wie lauten die Fragen? Ergänze.

1 _____'s your name? – Tim.

2 _____? – I'm eleven.

3 _____'s your house? – In Fairfield Road.

4 _____ lives in your house? – My family!

Yes, I do or **No, I don't?** Ergänze die Antworten.

1 Do you have your own room? – Yes, I _____.

2 Do you have a pet? – No, I _____.

3 Do you have a brother? – _____ – Peter.

4 Do you have a sister? – _____. She has a flat in London.

5 Do you have a flat too? – No, _____! I share a house with my family!

4 Sammy Vervollständige den Dialog mit Sammy.

1 What's _____? – Sammy.

2 How _____? – Very old!

3 Do you have a best friend? – _____, I do. It's Sarah.

4 _____ pet? – No, I don't! I **am** a pet.

5 _____ your own _____? – No, _____.

I share a room with Sarah. But I have a house in the room!

1 <u>**What do they have?**</u> **Schau dir die Zeichnungen an und trage die richtigen Wörter unten ein.**

1   The Millers have a _____, but they don't have a _____.

2   Pam has a _____, but she doesn't have a _____.

3   Mark has a _____, but he doesn't have a _____.

And you? What do you have?

I have a _____,

but I don't have a _____.

> Trage ein, was du hast und was du nicht hast.

2 <u>**Rosie and Tim**</u> **Wie viele Taschen, Füller und Bleistifte haben Rosie und Tim zusammen? Trage die Zahlen unten ein; die Summe muss 22 Gegenstände ergeben.**

Rosie has two bags. She doesn't have three bags. Tim has five bags. He doesn't have four bags. Rosie doesn't have two pencils. She has four pencils. Tim has eight pencils. He doesn't have six pencils. Rosie has one pen. She doesn't have three pens. Tim doesn't have five pens. He has two pens.

We have _____ bags,

_____ pencils and

_____ pens!

(= _____ things)

Reading and writing

1 A poem Lies das Gedicht.

Happy at home

I don't have a house,
I don't have a flat,
I don't have a bag
And my name is Pat.

I don't have a table,
I don't have a bed,
I don't have a cupboard
And my name is Fred.

I don't have a mum,
I don't have a dad,
I'm very, very old
And my name is Brad.

Tipp:
Beim Verständnis des Gedichtes helfen dir:
• der Titel,
• die Bilder,
• Wörter, die häufig wiederholt werden.

I don't have a room,
I don't have a pen,
I don't have a TV
And my name is Ben.

No, we don't have things,
We don't have toys *(Spielsachen)*,
We share a room
With girls and boys.

Beantworte nun die Fragen. Umkreise die richtigen Antworten.

1 Sprechen hier Jungen und Mädchen? – *Ja. / Nein.*

2 Sprechen hier Mütter und Väter? – *Ja. / Nein.*

3 Besitzen die Sprechenden viele Dinge? – *Ja. / Nein.*

4 Sind die Sprechenden traurig? – *Ja. / Nein.*

5 Was sind die Sprechenden? – *Haustiere. / Alte Menschen.*

2 And you? Schreibe über dich.

1 I'_____. (dein Alter)

2 I'm from _____. I _____ in _____.

3 _____ Schule. _____ year 5.

4 _____ my own room.

5 _____ a sister / ____ sisters.

6 _____ a brother / ____ brothers.

→ **Nützliche Wendungen:**
• I'm 10, 11, 12.
• I'm from Stuttgart/Bonn/…
• I live in Orffstraße/…
• I'm at … Schule.
• I'm in year …
• I have / don't have my own room / a sister / …

CHECK UNIT 1

Wie fit bist du nun? Alles im grünen Bereich?
Mache den Check und male dabei die Ampeln entsprechend aus.

1 Vocabulary Welche Wörter passen zusammen? Ziehe Linien.

1 table	new
2 kitchen	sister
3 brother	bathroom
4 nice	chair
5 house	terrible
6 old	flat

Lösungen: Seite 59

0–2 richtige Antworten: rot

3–4 richtige Antworten: gelb

5–6 richtige Antworten: grün

2 Communication Bringe die Wörter in den Fragen in die richtige Reihenfolge.

1 spider / have / you / a / Do   _____ ?

2 name / your / What's   _____ ?

3 your / colour / What / is / spider   _____ ?

4 lots of / Do you / friends / have   _____ ?

5 in / a TV / Do / have / you / your room   _____ ?

6 grandmas and grandads / have / you / Do   _____ ?

Lösungen: Seite 59

0–2 richtige Antworten: rot

3–4 richtige Antworten: gelb

5–6 richtige Antworten: grün

3 Practice Ergänze die Sätze mit den richtigen Wörtern aus dem Kasten.

1 Mark _____ a sister.

2 He _____ a brother.

3 Mark and his sister _____ a pet.

4 They _____ a hamster.

5 They _____ a spider.

6 He _____ a name – Harry.

• has (2x)
• have (2x)
• doesn't have
• don't have

Lösungen: Seite 60

0–2 richtige Antworten: rot

3–4 richtige Antworten: gelb

5–6 richtige Antworten: grün

4 Reading Lies zuerst den Text durch.

Hello, I'm a house!

I'm a house. My name is 2, Hill Road. I'm very big. I have a garden. It's a big garden. But I don't have a big kitchen. And the bathroom is terrible. It's very old. I'm a nice house, but I'm very old. My family has lots of work!

Nun umkreise die richtigen Wörter.

1 The *house* / *flat* is 2, Hill Road.

2 It's very old and *small* / *big*.

3 It doesn't have a big *garden* / *kitchen*.

4 The *kitchen* / *bathroom* is terrible.

5 It's a *terrible* / *nice* house.

6 The *family* / *house* has lots of work.

Lösungen: Seite 60

0–2 richtige Antworten: (rot)

3–4 richtige Antworten: (gelb)

5–6 richtige Antworten: (grün)

5 Writing Aysha möchte, dass du ihr bei einer E-Mail an ihre amerikanische Cousine hilfst. Schreibe die Sätze. Sie will sagen, dass ...

1 sie einen Bruder und eine Schwester hat: I _____.

2 sie in Konstanz wohnt: I _____.

3 sie in die Schillerschule geht: I _____.

4 sie kein eigenes Zimmer hat: I _____.

5 sie kein Haustier hat: I _____.

6 ihr Bruder eine Spinne hat: My _____.

Lösungen: Seite 60

0–2 richtige Antworten: (rot)

3–4 richtige Antworten: (gelb)

5–6 richtige Antworten: (grün)

1 Vocabulary

Bilde Gruppen von je drei Wörtern mit den passenden Wörtern aus dem Kasten.

1 chickens, _____, _____

2 cats, _____, _____

3 village, _____, _____

4 mother, _____, _____

5 get up, _____, _____

6 every day, _____, _____

- at eight o'clock
- come
- country
- dogs
- farm
- father
- go
- grandad
- hamsters
- pigs
- sheep
- usually

Lösungen: Seite 60   Weniger als fünf richtige Antworten → Seite 22 und 23

2 Communication

Wie lauten die Sätze? Verbinde die jeweils richtigen Hälften mit Linien.

1 I get up at   go home?

2 I play a game with   my quad.

3 I have   eight o'clock.

4 What do you   breakfast at half past eight.

5 I ride   dad.

6 When do you   do on Sundays?

Lösungen: Seite 60   Weniger als fünf richtige Antworten → Seite 24

3 Practice

Welche Wörter sind richtig? Umkreise sie.

1 I *go / goes* to bed at eight o'clock.

2 The bus *come / comes* at half past eight.

3 You *work / works* on the farm.

4 Tess *help / helps* with the sheep.

5 People *comes / come* to the shop.

6 Tess *watch / watches* the people.

Lösungen: Seite 60   Weniger als fünf richtige Antworten → Seite 25

4 Reading

Lies zuerst den Text durch.

Tom Green's day

Every day, on school days, Tom Green gets up at seven o'clock. He has breakfast at half past seven. He goes to school at eight o'clock. He talks to boys and girls. He comes home at four o'clock. He plays a game with Pam and Joe. Then he watches TV. It's "Waterloo Road School" at nine o'clock. He goes to bed at half past ten. He's a very tired teacher then!

***Yes* oder *No*? Setze ein ✔ in das richtige Kästchen.**

1 Tom Green gets up at eight o'clock. Yes. ☐ No. ☐
2 He has breakfast at half past seven. Yes. ☐ No. ☐
3 He goes to school at eight o'clock. Yes. ☐ No. ☐
4 He plays football at four o'clock. Yes. ☐ No. ☐
5 He watches TV with Pam and Joe. Yes. ☐ No. ☐
6 Tom Green is a boy. Yes. ☐ No. ☐

Lösungen: Seite 60   Weniger als fünf richtige Antworten ➜ Seite 26

5 Writing

Jim schildert seinem deutschen Freund in einer E-Mail seinen Tag. Schreibe die Sätze.

1 I _____ at half past _____.

2 I _____.

3 I _____.

4 I _____.

5 I _____.

6 I _____.

Lösungen: Seite 60   Weniger als fünf richtige Antworten ➜ Seite 26

1 **Animals** Finde die fehlenden Buchstaben und setze sie ein. Wenn du sie hintereinander schreibst, ergeben sie drei weitere Tiere.

shee___   bi___d   ___hicken

f___sh   c___t   h___rse

do___   hams___er

= ___ ___ ___   = ___ ___ ___   = ___ ___ w

2 **Find the words** Finde 10 Mehrzahl-Wörter (schau in zwei Richtungen: → und ↓) und schreibe sie unten auf. Trage sie dabei in die richtige Spalte ein.

→ 6 Wörter
↓ 4 Wörter

```
H E R H I P L O U Y T R I N G
L S E Y B R O C H I C K E N S
G F F I S H V O T M N X I S T
Z S P R T I D U M O R L P E V
I D I C T I O N A R I E S C I
O C H A N Y R T G U D F T O L
A W E E C H O R S E S B O H L
T C O W S A D I K L H U R N A
C G R O U S A E W H E L I N G
F A M I L I E S B U E T E Y E
N E D F P O L R T A P S S D S
```

1 Mehrzahl mit –s	2 Mehrzahl mit –ies	3 Mehrzahl unverändert
_____	_____	_____
_____	_____	_____
_____	_____	_____
_____	_____	_____

3 **My school days** Ergänze die Sätze mit passenden Verben. Die Buchstaben dafür sind alle unten aufgeführt.

1   Every morning I _____ up at half past six.

2   I _____ breakfast.

3   I _____ to school at seven.

4   I _____ home at two o'clock.

5   I _____ my homework.

6   Then I _____ with my friends.

7   I _____ TV.

8   I usually _____ to bed at ten o'clock.

4 **When and where?** Welche Begriffe haben etwas mit einer Zeitangabe zu tun? Welche mit einer Ortsangabe? Schreibe die Begriffe in die beiden Listen und addiere die angegebenen Punkte. Stimmt die Summe mit der Lösungssumme überein?

Zeit	Ort
_____	_____
_____	_____
_____	_____
_____	_____
_____	_____
_____ (=30)	_____ (=25)

→
- every day (4)
- at the window (2)
- to the shop (7)
- half past six (3)
- in the country (1)
- near Kenn (5)
- usually (8)
- after school (6)
- at eight o'clock (9)
- on the farm (10)

TRAIN UNIT 2 Communication

1 On Saturdays Bringe die Wörter in die richtige Reihenfolge.

1 at ten o'clock / get up / I _____.

2 breakfast / have / at half past ten / I _____.

3 with my friends / I / play _____.

4 to / a big shop / I / go _____.

5 TV / watch / I _____.

> Tipp:
> Alle Sätze fangen mit I an. Darauf folgt ein Verb.

2 Questions Wie lauten die Fragen?

→ **Nützliche Wörter: on Saturdays** · on Sundays get up · go to school · come home

Frage Tom bitte, ...

1 wann er aufsteht: _____?

2 wann er zur Schule geht: _____?

3 wann er nach Hause kommt: _____?

4 was er samstags macht: _____?

5 was er sonntags macht: _____?

3 What's right? Welche Wörter sind richtig? Umkreise sie.

1 On school days I *get up / go to bed* at seven o'clock.

2 On *Saturdays / school days* I go to bed late.

3 On Sundays I *have breakfast / come home* at 11 o'clock.

4 On Saturdays I *ride my quad bike / go to school*.

5 On school days I come home at *half past four / half past eight*.

6 On Sundays I play games with my *teachers / friends*.

4 A dialogue Vervollständige den Dialog.

1 _____ on school days? – I go to school!

2 _____ go to school? – At half past eight.

3 _____ after school? – My homework!

4 What do you _____ homework? – _____ TV.

5 What do you _____ TV? _____ to bed!

6 What do you do after bed? _____ school!

1 **Who?** Ordne die Personen aus dem Kasten den Bildern und Sätzen zu.

→ **grandma** · Kevin · mum · the Browns

Every day at eight o'clock ...

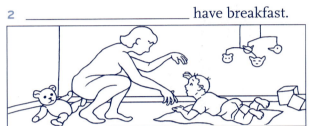

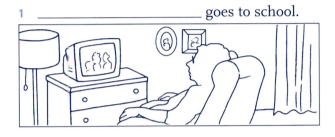

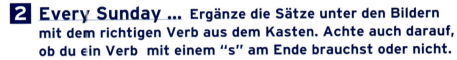

1 _____ goes to school.

2 _____ have breakfast.

3 _____ watches TV.

4 _____ plays with Rosie.

2 **Every Sunday ...** Ergänze die Sätze unter den Bildern mit dem richtigen Verb aus dem Kasten. Achte auch darauf, ob du ein Verb mit einem "s" am Ende brauchst oder nicht.

→ **comes** · get · go · plays read · ride · watches

1 Every Sunday we

_____ up late.

2 After breakfast I

_____ my bike.

3 My brother _____

with our dog.

4 Every Sunday afternoon

my grandma _____.

5 Then my brother

_____ TV and I

_____.

6 We usually _____

to bed early.

Das "s" am Ende des Verbs kann dir zeigen, mit welcher Person es benutzt wird.

1 **Who am I?** Lies die Aussagen und errate dann die Namen.

1
I go to the bus.
I help with the sheep.
I watch the people in the shop.
I wait for the bus.

My name is _____.

2
I live with my mum and dad.
I ride my quad bike on Saturdays.
I live in the country.
I live near Kenn.

My name is _____.

3
I have a small farm.
I have sheep and chickens.
I work in the farm shop.

My name is _____.

> Tipp:
> Folgende Menschen werden gesucht: Jamie, Sarah, Mrs Fraser, Mr Fraser. Auch ein Tier wird gesucht!

> Tipp:
> Wenn du unsicher bist, schau noch einmal in Unit 2 in deinem Buch nach.

4
I play football on Saturdays.
I read and I watch TV.
I ride my bike.
I play with Sammy.

My name is _____.

5
I live in the country.
I have a small farm.
I work on the farm.
I have a boy – Jamie.

My name is _____.

2 **Pat** Schreibe über Pats Tag.

1   I get up _____.

2   I _____ at half past seven.

3   I go to school _____.

4   I come home _____.

5   Then I  _____ with my brother.

6   I usually _____

     at _____

> Tipp:
> **um** sechs Uhr = **at** six o'clock
> Keine s-Endung bei den Verben!
> Denn alle Sätze fangen mit I an.

CHECK ~~UNIT~~ 2

Wie fit bist du nun? Alles im grünen Bereich?
Mache den Check und male dabei die Ampeln entsprechend aus.

1 Vocabulary Welches Wort passt nicht in die Reihe? Streiche es durch.

1 chickens, pigs, dogs, cows

2 cats, dogs, sheep, hamsters

3 wheelchair, car, bus, animal

4 watch, get up, come, go

5 on Saturdays, usually, play, every day

6 country, town, farm, breakfast

Lösungen: Seite 61

0–2 richtige Antworten: rot

3–4 richtige Antworten: gelb

5–6 richtige Antworten: grün

2 Communication Bringe die Wörter in die richtige Reihenfolge.

1 my / I / homework / do _____.

2 quac / I / my / ride / bike _____.

3 with / play / I / Sammy _____.

4 with / I / play / games / friends / my _____.

5 at / I / help / home

_____.

6 at / I / seven o'clock / get up

_____.

Lösungen: Seite 61

0–2 richtige Antworten: rot

3–4 richtige Antworten: gelb

5–6 richtige Antworten: grün

3 Practice Setze die fehlenden Wörter ein.

1 Tess and Jamie g_____ to the bus.

2 Tess w_____ on the farm.

3 She h_____ with the sheep.

4 Tess g_____ to the road every afternoon.

5 She w_____ for the bus.

6 Then Tess and Jamie g_____ home.

Lösungen: Seite 62

0–2 richtige Antworten: rot

3–4 richtige Antworten: gelb

5–6 richtige Antworten: grün

4 Reading Lies zuerst den Text durch.

Tim

I'm Tim. I'm a dog. I live near Kenn. I live near Jamie's dog, Tess. She's a great dog. But she works and works and works! She works on the farm and in the shop. I wait for Tess every afternoon. But she waits for Jamie and then they go home!

Nun umkreise die richtigen Wörter.

1 Tim *lives / works* near Kenn.

2 *She's / He's* a dog.

3 Tim says *Tess / Jamie* is great.

4 Tim says Tess *plays / works* every day.

5 Tim waits for Tess every *afternoon / morning*.

6 Tess waits for *Tim / Jamie*.

Lösungen: Seite 62

0–2 richtige Antworten: rot
3–4 richtige Antworten: gelb
5–6 richtige Antworten: grün

5 Writing Hilf Anna dabei, ihrer australischen Cousine eine Mail auf Englisch zu schreiben.

Sie will sagen, dass ...

1 sie um sieben Uhr aufsteht: I _____.

2 sie um halb acht zur Schule geht: I _____.

3 sie Fußball spielt: I _____.

4 sie mit ihrem Bruder fernsieht: I _____.

5 sie gewöhnlich "Eurostars" sieht: I _____.

6 sie um neun Uhr ins Bett geht: I _____.

Lösungen: Seite 62

0–2 richtige Antworten: rot
3–4 richtige Antworten: gelb
5–6 richtige Antworten: grün

TEST UNIT 3

1 Vocabulary

Put in the missing words.

1 sports centre, park, sw_____ p_____

2 day, week, m_____

3 fish and chip shop, supermarket, p_____ shop

4 go swimming, go canoeing, go d_____

5 me, him, h_____

6 lesson, school, cl_____

Lösungen: Seite 62   Weniger als fünf richtige Antworten ➜ *Seite 31 und 32*

2 Communication

Welche Sätze gehören zusammen? Ziehe Linien.

1 I like dogs.	It's a terrible place.
2 I like football.	It's a terrible sport.
3 I like "Eurostars".	It's great.
4 I don't like cats.	They're boring.
5 I don't like tennis.	They're great.
6 I don't like school.	It's a good sport.

Lösungen: Seite 62   Weniger als fünf richtige Antworten ➜ *Seite 33*

3 Practice

Which is the right word? Put in *doesn't* or *don't*.

1 Our house _____ have a garden.

2 I _____ like football.

3 My dad _____ play games.

4 I _____ live near the town centre.

5 My brother _____ want a dog.

6 My mum _____ live with us.

Lösungen: Seite 62   Weniger als fünf richtige Antworten ➜ *Seite 34*

4 Reading

Read the text.

Monty

Hello. I'm Nikki's dog. My name is Monty. I'm three months old. I like magazines. I **eat** magazines! I often go to the park. I like the park. But I don't walk next to Nikki. I don't come. I don't sit. And I don't like cats! I'm a nice dog. But I'm lots of work!

Right or wrong? Put a ✔ in the right box.

1 Monty is three months old.   Right. ☐   Wrong. ☐

2 He "eats" magazines.   Right. ☐   Wrong. ☐

3 He doesn't like the park.   Right. ☐   Wrong. ☐

4 He walks next to Nikki.   Right. ☐   Wrong. ☐

5 He doesn't come and he doesn't sit.   Right. ☐   Wrong. ☐

6 He likes cats.   Right. ☐   Wrong. ☐

Lösungen: Seite 62   Weniger als fünf richtige Antworten ➜ Seite 35

5 Writing

Ben's e-mail to his English friend: Finish the sentences.

1 I _____ football.

2 I _____.

3 I _____.

4 I _____ like _____.

5 I _____.

6 I _____.

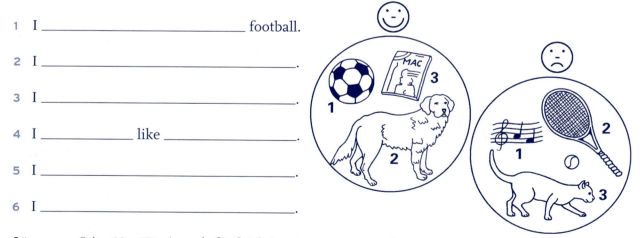

Lösungen: Seite 62   Weniger als fünf richtige Antworten ➜ Seite 35

1 Crossword Put in the English words.

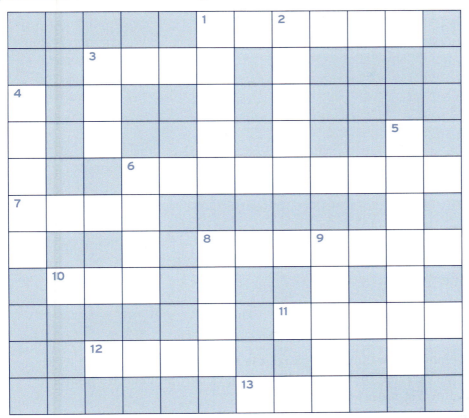

Waagerecht →
1 sportlich
3 Ball
6 teuer
7 Idee
8 Geschenk
10 Spielzeug
11 jung
12 gehen, laufen
13 essen; fressen

Senkrecht ↓
1 schlafen
2 oft
3 kaufen
4 Musik
5 Abend
6 einfach, leicht
8 Park
9 Sport, Sportart

2 The right word Finde das richtige Personalpronomen (Frage: Wem oder wen?) zu jedem Bild und trage es unten in die Kästchen ein. Es entsteht ein neues Lösungswort, mit dem du Sammys Sprechblase ergänzen kannst.

1 Pat: "Let's play with ___ ___ ___ ."

2 Jack: "I can help ___ ___ ___ !"

3 Sally: "I like ___ ___ ___ ."

4 Kitty: "He can't find ___ ___ here!"

Our new ___ ___ ___ ___ is in Alphington.

3 **Partners** Welche Wortbestandteile ergeben zusammen ein neues Wort? Ziehe Linien.

1   clothes   centre

2   youth

> Zu einem der Wörter müssen **fünf** Linien führen.

3   pet   club

4   fish and chip

5   sports   market

6   book

7   super   pool

8   swimming

9   CD   shop

4 **I can't!** Schau dir die Zeichnungen an und ergänze die richtigen Verben in den Kästchen. Trage die Buchstaben aus den markierten Kästchen in der gleichen Reihenfolge unten in das Lückenwort ein. Wie lautet das Lösungswort?

1   She can't ☐☐☐ it.

2   He can't ☐☐☐ it.

3   I can't ☐☐☐☐☐ !

4   We can't ☐☐☐☐☐ !

5   They can't ☐☐☐☐ .

6   Sorry, I can't ☐☐☐ you.

Lösungswort:

| Q | | | | T | I | O | | N | | I | R | |

1 Tina Tina mag keine Tiere. Sie mag alle Sportarten. Was sagt sie?

1 I _____ dogs.

2 I _____ football.

3 I _____ tennis.

4 I _____ cats.

> Tipp:
> mögen = *I like*
> nicht mögen =
> *I don't like*

2 ... and Bob Bob mag gar nichts!

1 Sundays – boring: I don't like Sundays. They're boring.

2 football – dangerous: I _____ . It's _____ .

3 pets – lots of work: _____ . _____ .

4 "Teen Music Scene" – terrible: _____ . _____ .

3 Pete and Paul Paul macht nichts, was Pete macht. Was sagt Paul?

1 Pete: I buy CDs. Paul: I don't _____ .

2 Pete: I watch "Teen Music Scene". Paul: I don't _____ .

3 Pete: I like football. Paul: _____ .

4 Pete: I eat hamburgers. Paul: _____ .

4 New friends? Finish the dialogue.

1 I like English. What about you? – _____ English. It's terrible.

2 I like cats. _____ ? – I don't like cats.

3 And I like dogs. What about you? – _____ . They're boring.

4 Dogs? Boring?! I don't like football matches. – I _____ football matches. They're great!

5 You like football matches?? Boring! – And I like _____ .

6 Sports magazines?? I watch "Teen Music Scene". – I _____ too!

Come to my house.
We can watch it.
You like it and I like it!!!

1 **That isn't right! But what *is* right?** Welche beiden Sätze gehören jeweils
zusammen? Ziehe Linien und trage die Buchstaben hinter den Sätzen unten ein.
Wenn du alles richtig hast, ergibt sich ein Wort aus dieser Unit.

1 Sharon doesn't have a cat.   They live in London. (P)

2 The Millers don't live in Exeter.   He buys music magazines. (R)

3 I don't play football.   We go swimming. (T)

4 My brother doesn't buy sports magazines.   She has a dog. (S)

5 We don't go dancing.   You get up early. (Y)

6 You don't get up late on Sundays.   I play tennis. (O)

1	2	3	4	5	6

2 **People** Schau dir an, was die Personen mögen (✔) und was sie nicht mögen (✗).
Wähle dann die passenden Satzanfänge und schreibe drei Steckbriefe.

	cats	dogs	music	reading	basketball	volleyball
Aysha	✗	✗	✔	✗	✔	✗
Kevin	✗	✔	✔	✗	✗	✔
Ben and Tim	✔	✗	✗	✔	✔	✗

1 Aysha _____.

_____.

2 Kevin _____.

_____.

3 Ben and Tim _____.

_____.

Aysha / Kevin / She / He =
likes • doesn't like …
Ben and Tim / They = *like • don't like …*

1 **A questionnaire** Read the questionnaire.

Do you have a good dog?

Name: *Mike Lee*
Dog's name: *Sandy*
How old? *3 months*

Answer Yes or No.

A		B	
My dog bites me.	*No.*	My dog walks next to me.	*No.*
My dog eats magazines.	*Yes.*	My dog comes.	*No.*
My dog takes my things.	*No.*	My dog sits.	*Yes.*
My dog often barks.	*Yes.*	My dog likes cats.	*Yes.*
My dog sleeps in my bed.	*No.*	My dog is fun.	*Yes.*

A: 2x *Yes* and **B:** 2x *No*: Your dog is OK. You have an easy, but not a **very** easy, life.

Umkreise nun die jeweils richtigen Wörter.

1   Mike's dog *bites / doesn't bite* him.

2   Sandy *eats / doesn't eat* magazines.

3   Sandy *takes / doesn't take* Mike's things.

4   He *walks / doesn't walk* next to Mike.

5   He *comes / doesn't come*.

6   He *likes / doesn't like* cats.

> Tipp:
> *no = doesn't + Verb*
> *yes = nur das Verb*

2 **And Meg?** Write the sentences for her.

1   read   I read _____.

2   ~~read~~   I don't _____.

3   play   I _____.

4   ~~play~~   I _____.

5   ~~buy~~   I _____.

6   buy   I _____.

Wie fit bist du nun? Alles im grünen Bereich?
Mache den Check und male dabei die Ampeln entsprechend aus.

1 Vocabulary Put the words from the box in the right lines.

1 shops: _____, _____, _____

2 places: _____, _____, _____

3 words about people: _____, _____, _____

4 (lots of) days: _____, _____, _____

5 verbs: _____, _____, _____

6 words for people: _____, _____, _____

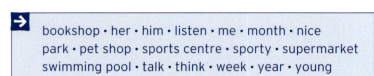

bookshop · her · him · listen · me · month · nice
park · pet shop · sports centre · sporty · supermarket
swimming pool · talk · think · week · year · young

Lösungen: Seite 64

0–2 richtige Antworten: (rot)

3–4 richtige Antworten: (gelb)

5–6 richtige Antworten: (grün)

2 Communication Make sentences from Sally's notes. What doesn't she do/like? Why...?

1 ~~watch TV~~ – boring   I _____. _____.

2 ~~play football~~ – terrible   I _____. _____.

3 ~~buy CDs~~ – expensive   I _____. _____.

4 ~~like dogs~~ – dangerous   I _____. _____.

5 ~~like hamsters~~ – dirty   I _____.

_____.

6 ~~read comics~~ – boring   I _____.

_____.

Lösungen: Seite 64

0–2 richtige Antworten: (rot)

3–4 richtige Antworten: (gelb)

5–6 richtige Antworten: (grün)

3 Practice Rod geht es nicht so gut wie Rob. Was sagt Rod?

1 Rob: My dad plays games.   Rod: My dad _____ play games.

2 Rob: My sisters help me with homework.   Rod: My sisters _____.

_____.

3 Rob: My mum buys me magazines.   Rod: My mum _____.

Fortsetzung S. 37 →

4 Rob: I have my own room. Rod: I _____.

5 Rob: We live in a big house. Rod: We _____

_____.

6 Rob: My friends live near me. Rod: My friends _____

_____.

4 Reading Read the text.

Tiddles

I'm Tiddles. I'm a cat. I'm six months old. I like my people.
They're very nice. I like fish. I eat lots of fish. I'm not a dog,
so I don't walk next to people. I don't come. But I sit. I sit on
beds. I like beds! I'm a nice cat. And I'm not lots of work!

Right, wrong or not in the text? Put a ✔ in the right box.

	Right.	Wrong.	Not in the text.
1 Tiddles is six months old.	☐	☐	☐
2 She doesn't like old people.	☐	☐	☐
3 She doesn't eat lots of fish.	☐	☐	☐
4 She comes.	☐	☐	☐
5 She sits on beds.	☐	☐	☐
6 She doesn't like dogs.	☐	☐	☐

5 Writing Write Annika's e-mail to her English cousin.

Sie will sagen, dass ...

1 sie Hunde mag: I _____.

2 sie keine Katzen mag: I _____.

3 sie viele Zeitschriften kauft: I _____.

4 sie keine CDs kauft: I _____.

5 sie Tennis spielt: I _____

_____.

6 sie keinen Fußball spielt: I _____

_____.

1 Vocabulary

Where can you find this things/people? Draw lines.

1	car		airport
2	money		farm
3	plane		bike
4	canoe		bank
5	farmer		car park
6	light		river

Lösungen: Seite 64   Weniger als fünf richtige Antworten → Seite 40 und 41

2 Communication

Draw lines.

1	Do you often		a favourite football team?
2	Do your sisters		brother live at home?
3	Does your mum watch		to play a game?
4	Do you have		ride your bike?
5	Do you want		quiz shows on TV?
6	Does your		like football?

Lösungen: Seite 64   Weniger als fünf richtige Antworten → Seite 42

3 Practice

Put in _Do_ or _Does_.

1 _____ your dad play with you?

2 _____ you like football?

3 _____ your mum work in a bank?

4 _____ your friends buy CDs?

5 _____ your dog walk next to you?

6 _____ I ask too many questions?

Lösungen: Seite 64   Weniger als fünf richtige Antworten → Seite 43

4 Reading

Read the text.

Jane Brown and her bike

Jane Brown rides her bike every day. She likes her bike. It's a mountain bike. Her mum is a road safety trainer. She always has lots of questions for Jane. "Do you ride on the pavement? Do you use bike tracks? Do you give hand signals?" Jane always gives the right answer. She knows what answers road safety trainers want!

Now put in the missing words.

1 Jane Brown often _____ her bike.

2 She likes her _____.

3 Her mum is a road safety _____.

4 Mrs Brown asks, "Do you give _____ signals?"

5 Jane always gives the _____ answer.

6 She knows what _____ road safety trainers want!

Lösungen: Seite 64   Weniger als fünf richtige Antworten ➜ Seite 44

5 Writing

What does the road safety trainer write about Rachel?
Put in the missing words.

1  She _____ give hand _____.

2 She _____ use bike _____.

3  She rides _____ pavement.

4 She _____ have _____ on her bike.

5 She _____ stop _____ traffic lights.

6 She can have her first road safety _____ next week!

Lösungen: Seite 64   Weniger als fünf richtige Antworten ➜ Seite 44

1 <u>**Odd word out**</u> **Den folgenden Wörtern fehlt in jeder Reihe ein bestimmter Buchstabe. Setze ihn ein. Dann betrachte die Wörter. Welches passt nicht in die Reihe? Füge diese Wörter unten zu einem Satz zusammen.**

Tipp: Achte auf die Wortart: Wo hat sich z. B. ein Adjektiv zwischen die Nomen geschmuggelt?

1   st__p · f__rget · sh__uted · __ur

2   bette__ · mode__n · fa__m · elect__onic

3   par__nts · v__ry · driv__r · farm__r

4   tra__ · __oney · __odern · __otorbike

Jamie: "(1) _____ (2) _____ is (3) _____ (4) _____ !"

2 <u>**What? Where?**</u> **Put in the missing words.**

1   You can find p_____

    at the a_____ ...

2   ... and _____

    on the c_____ _____.

3   There are _____

    on the b_____ ...

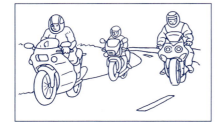

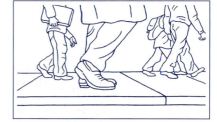

4   ... and _____

    on the _____.

5   Jamie rides his

    m_____ _____

    off-road.

6   And I go _____ _____.

    I use the p_____.

3 Partners Schau dir die folgenden Wörter an und schreibe die 6 Wortpaare, die sich reimen, auf. Vorsicht: Du brauchst nicht alle Wörter aus dem Kasten!

→ bark • black • bring • give • light • line • plane • sign
sport • spring • thought • track • train • tram • write

Tipp: Sprich die Wörter laut aus!

_____ – _____   _____ – _____

_____ – _____   _____ – _____

_____ – _____   _____ – _____

way   say

4 Football fans Ergänze das richtige Verb in den Sätzen der Geschichte. Dann übertrage die Verben an die richtige Stelle im Kreuzworträtsel unten und überprüfe, ob alles passt.

→ • saw
• shouted
• thought
• wanted
• went (2x)
• were (2x)

1   Mark (2) _____ to London at the weekend.

2   He (3 ↓) _____ to see the football match.

3   There (3 →) _____ lots of football fans in London.

4   They (3 →) _____ terrible. They (1 ↓) _____: "Chelsea! Chelsea!"

5   But Mark is an Exeter fan! He (4) _____: "I have to get out of this place."

6   He (2) _____ home and (1 →) _____ the match there – it was on TV!

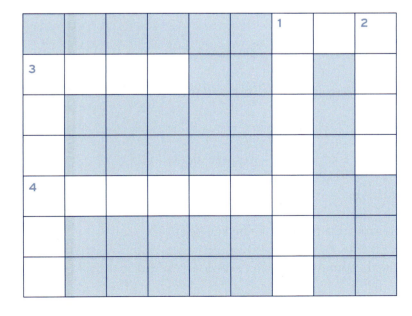

STADIUM

1 **Bob and his questions** Write the questions.

1 to the swimming pool / Do you / go   _____?

2 play / want to / football / Do you   _____?

3 to my new CD / Do you / want to / listen   _____?

4 cats and dogs / Do you / like   _____?

2 **Matt and his answers** Match the answers in the box with the questions in 1. Write them on the right line and put in do or don't.

→
- Yes, I … . I like *The Huggers*.
- Yes, I … . They're great pets.
- Yes, I … . Swimming is great.
- No, I … . I don't like football.

1 *Yes, I do. Swimming is great.* _____

2 _____

3 _____

4 _____

3 **More questions** Draw lines.

1 Does your dad like   to your house?

2 Does your mum often see   with cats?

3 Does your brother live   his job?

4 Do your friends come   magazines for you?

5 Do your mum and dad buy   her friends?

6 Does your dog play   in a new flat?

4 **Terrible Terry** Finish the dialogue.

1 Does your mum have a job? – Yes, _____. She works at the tourist information.

2 _____ dad _____ at the tourist information too?

3 – _____. He works at a bank.

4 Does _____ like people? – Yes, she does.

5 _____ the people ask lots of questions? – Yes, they do. And mum always has the answer.

6 _____ help people from Exeter too? – Yes, she does.

7 _____ pupils with homework? – No, she doesn't. You're terrible, Terry!

42

1 **Questions with _Yes/No_ answers** Finde die richtigen Antworten auf die Fragen und ziehe Linien. Notiere den jeweiligen Lösungsbuchstaben unten in der richtigen Reihenfolge, und du erhältst ein Wort aus dieser Unit.

1 Do you get to school on foot?   No, they don't. (V)

2 Does your brother like motorbikes?   Yes, she does. (I)

3 Does your sister always use bike tracks?   Yes, I do. (D)

4 Do your parents often go to work by train?   Yes, we do. (R)

5 Does your bike have lights?   No, he doesn't. (R)

6 Do we have to do our homework?   Yes, it does. (E)

___ ___ ___ ___ ___ ___
 1   2   3   4   5   6

2 **Who likes what?** Write 7 questions with _Do/Does._

> Tipp: Die Antworten helfen dir bei der Auswahl zwischen _Do_ und _Does_!

	you		his room? – No, **he doesn't.** It's too small.
	Tim		her class? – Yes, **she does.** The pupils are OK.
Do	the pupils		your dog? – Yes, **I do.** Rocky is great!
Does	Ms Brown	like	their teacher? – Yes, **they do.** She's nice.
	Mr Fraser		their car? – No, **they don't.** It's too old.
	Pam		his farm? – Yes, **he does.** It's modern.
	the Millers		her brother? – No, **she doesn't.** He's terrible!

1 _____?

2 _____?

3 _____?

4 _____?

5 _____?

6 _____?

7 _____?

1 **Jobs** Lies die Stellenangebote durch. Um welche der unten genannten Stellen handelt es sich jeweils? Schreibe die richtigen Buchstaben in die Kästchen unten.

A Help people from other places. Answer their questions.	**E** Explain things to children at school.
B Work with money, lots of money!	**F** Explain things to children on bikes.
C Deal with people's bags.	**G** Work with animals and in fields.
D Drive lots of people to places.	**H** Do you play the guitar? "The Hobies" want you!

1 teacher ☐
2 farmer ☐
3 bus driver ☐
4 baggage handler ☐

5 a job in a tourist information ☐
6 a job in a band ☐
7 road safety trainer ☐
8 a job in a bank ☐

2 **Questions** Find the partners and write 6 questions.

1 Do your friends   her clothes in Exeter?
2 Does your sister buy   your best friend?
3 Are you   with **his** job?
4 Is your dad happy   often in the park with your friends?
5 Can you   always do **their** homework?
6 Am I   come with us, please?

Tipp: Achte auf die **fetten** Wörter. Sie helfen dir bei der Zuordnung.
his = eine Person (männlich)
her = eine Person (weiblich)
their = mehrere Personen

1 _____

2 _____

3 _____

4 _____

5 _____

6 _____

CHECK UNIT 4

Wie fit bist du nun? Alles im grünen Bereich?
Mache den Check und male dabei die Ampeln entsprechend aus.

1 **Vocabulary** Ergänze jede Wortgruppe mit dem passenden
Wort aus dem Kasten.

- baggage handler
- electronic
- his
- street
- train
- wanted

1 motorbike, bike, car, _____

2 fast, quiet, modern, _____

3 driver, farmer, teacher, _____

4 my, her, their, _____

5 saw, went, thought, _____

6 pavement, track, road, _____

Lösungen: Seite 66

0–2 richtige Antworten:	rot
3–4 richtige Antworten:	gelb
5–6 richtige Antworten:	grün

2 **Communication** Make questions. Use the notes.

1 your dad – have a job   D_____ your dad have a job?

2 your brothers – live at home   D_____?

3 your mum – work at the bank   D_____?

4 your friends – watch TV   D_____?

5 you – like Chelsea   D_____?

6 your teachers – live near the school   D_____?

3 **Practice** Make the questions.

1 _____ you want a new bag?

2 _____ your dog walk next to you?

3 _____ your mum and dad work?

4 _____ your teacher live in Exeter?

5 _____ farmers like mountain bikes?

6 _____ the track go to Kenn?

Lösungen: Seite 66

0–2 richtige Antworten:	rot
3–4 richtige Antworten:	gelb
5–6 richtige Antworten:	grün

Lösungen: Seite 66

0–2 richtige Antworten:	rot
3–4 richtige Antworten:	gelb
5–6 richtige Antworten:	grün

4 Reading Read the text.

No place like home

Pepper is four years old. He's Tom Price's cat. Tom's dad is a baggage handler at Exeter airport. Pepper often goes to the airport with him. (Mr Price doesn't know this!) Pepper goes in the planes. He goes to nice places. But he always comes home in the evening. Pepper likes his home. And Tom is a good friend. He feeds Pepper with nice things. Pepper says it's nice to go to places, but there's no place like home!

"No place like home"

One thing is wrong in every line.
Cross it out and write the right words.

1   Pepper is Tom Price's dog.   _____

2   Pepper often goes to the shops.   _____

3   Mr Price knows this.   _____

4   Pepper goes in the trains.   _____

5   He often comes home in the evening. _____

6   Pepper says there's no place like school. _____

Lösungen: Seite 66.

0–2 richtige Antworten: (rot)

3–4 richtige Antworten: (gelb)

5–6 richtige Antworten: (grün)

5 Writing Help Julia with her e-mail to her English mail partner. Write the questions in English.

Sie will ihre E-Mail-Freundin fragen, ob ...

1   sie Fußball mag: _____ ?

2   sie oft fernsieht: _____ ?

3   sie ein Haustier hat: _____ ?

4   ihre Mutter eine Stelle hat: _____ ?

5   ihr Bruder zu Hause wohnt: _____ ?

6   sie viele E-Mails schreibt: _____ ?

Lösungen: Seite 66.

0–2 richtige Antworten: (rot)

3–4 richtige Antworten:

5–6 richtige Antworten:

TEST UNIT 5

1 Vocabulary

Ergänze jede Wortgruppe mit dem passenden Wort aus dem Kasten.

→ | August · beach · evening · ice cream · milk · orange |

1 summer, sun, _____

4 morning, afternoon, _____

2 banana, apple, _____

5 cola, juice, _____

3 June, July, _____

6 cake, chocolate, _____

Lösungen: Seite 66   Weniger als fünf richtige Antworten → Seite 49 und 50

2 Communication

Find the right answer to every question. draw lines.

1 When's your birthday?   Yes, please – great!

2 What are you doing on your birthday?   Paul, Tim, all my friends.

3 Who are you inviting?   I'm helping mum this evening.

4 What are you doing this evening?   Next Saturday? I'm not sure.

5 What are you doing next Saturday?   It's in July.

6 Do you want to come to Jamie's farm?   I'm having a party.

Lösungen: Seite 66   Weniger als fünf richtige Antworten → Seite 51

3 Practice

Bilde die richtige Form des Verbs in Klammern.

Example: (go) Lots of people ... on holiday next week.
→ Lots of people are going on holiday next week.

1 (stay) I_____ here in the holidays.

2 (stay) Kevin _____ at home too.

3 (have) My friend _____ a party.

4 (go) We_____ to the cinema.

5 (visit) Next week the girls _____ their grandma.

6 (go) You_____ to England next month.

Lösungen: Seite 67   Weniger als fünf richtige Antworten → Seite 52

4 Reading

Read the text.

Jim's birthday party

It's Jim's birthday next week and he's having a big party. All his friends are coming. They're having a picnic in Jim's garden with cake and cola, ice cream and orange juice. Jim wants to play football and listen to music too. Jim's dog is a problem. He can't go in the garden with all the cakes and ice cream! And here's a very big problem: Jim's parents don't know about the party!

Now (circle) the right words.

1   It's Jim's birthday next *month / week*.

2   He's having a *big / small* party.

3   The party is *in Jim's garden / at the beach*.

4   Jim wants to *go swimming / play football*.

5   Jim's dog *is / isn't* a problem.

6   Jim's parents *know / don't know* about the party.

Lösungen: Seite 67   Weniger als fünf richtige Antworten ➜ Seite 53

5 Writing

Make sentences. Use the notes.

1   we – go – Spain – for two weeks   We're _____.

2   I – not – go – on holiday – this year   I'm not _____.

3   stay – at home – holidays   I'm _____.

4   visit – grandma and old friends   I'm _____.

5   my birthday – July   It's _____.

6   big party – 7 o'clock   I'm _____.

Lösungen: Seite 67   Weniger als fünf richtige Antworten ➜ Seite 53

1 The third word Ergänze jede Reihe mit dem passenden Wort aus dem Kasten. Schreibe den gesuchten Lösungsbuchstaben hinter die Zeile.

→ August · banana · chocolate milk · museum · sea · Spain

1 orange – apple – _____ (3. Buchstabe: __)   1

2 June – July – _____ (1. Buchstabe: __)   2

3 tea – juice – _____ (2. Buchstabe: __)   3

4 sun – beach – _____ (1. Buchstabe: __)   4

5 England – Germany – _____ (2. Buchstabe: __)   5

6 cinema – cafe – _____ (4. Buchstabe: __)   6

7 ice cream – cake – _____ (1. Buchstabe: __)   7

Trage jetzt die Lösungsbuchstaben an der richtigen Stelle ein, und du erhältst ein weiteres Wort aus der Unit:

__ H __ __ R __ __ R __ O __
7   2 3   5 6   4   1

2 What is it? Suche das passende Wort aus dieser Unit.

Tipp: Die Buchstaben rechts sind die Anfangsbuchstaben der gesuchten Wörter.

1 a place for pictures: _____

2 a place for a holiday: _____

3 a place for films: _____

4 a place for trains: _____

5 a place for ice cream and cake: _____

6 a place for fun in the sun: _____

3 __What are the questions?__ Suche die richtigen Verben (links) und Nomen (rechts) aus den Kästen und ergänze die Fragen unten.

→   get · go · have · invite · stay · visit

→   dad · friends · holiday · holiday flat · party · tea

1   Can you _____ me my _____, please?

2   Can I _____ a birthday _____?

3   Can we _____ at a _____ this summer?

4   Can we _____ on _____ soon?

5   Can I _____ my _____ to our party?

6   Can I _____ at the weekend?

4 __Crossword__ Put in the English words.

		1	2				3	4			
5				6						7	
8											
					9		10				
	11										
							12				
	13										

Waagerecht →

1   bald
3   andere, weitere
6   Picknick
8   Plan
10   Sonne
11   Wetter
12   Mai
13   Überraschung

Senkrecht ↓

2   Orange, Apfelsine
4   Ausflug, Reise
5   Apfel
6   Postkarte, Ansichtskarte
7   Spaß
9   Meer
10   Sommer

1 **When's your birthday?** Was sagen die Kinder? Ergänze die Antworten.

1 (Leo) – It's in A_____ . (8.)

2 (Pat) _____ . (7.)

3 (Dave) _____ . (1.)

4 (Tim) _____ . (3.)

5 (Sally) _____ . (6.)

> Tipps: Alle Sätze fangen gleich an. Jeder Monat hat eine Ordnungszahl, z. B. 1. = Januar, 12. = Dezember

2 **What are their plans?** Bringe die Wörter in die richtige Reihenfolge.

1 with mum / going to town / I'm   _____ .

2 in the kitchen / dad / helping / I'm   _____ .

3 with Tom / I'm / football / playing   _____ .

4 a big party / next week / I'm / having   _____ .

5 I'm / my friends / to the party / inviting   _____ .

3 **Questions** Draw lines.

1 When's   are you inviting to your party?

2 What   want to come to town with me?

3 Who   are you going next weekend?

4 Where   your birthday?

5 Do you   are you doing on Saturday?

4 **Terrible** Finish the dialogue.

1 What _____ this evening?

2 – I'm not sure. Do you _____ "Teen Time" with me?

3 No, thank you! _____ doing n_____ Saturday?

4 – _____ to my grandma's house.

Do you want to come with me?

5 No, thank you! Boring! And _____ about next Saturday?

6 – _____ a party. And you aren't coming!

> Tipp: Sieh dir die anderen Sätze dieser Übung an, wenn du unsicher bist. Sie enthalten nützliche Informationen!

1 **This summer ...** Put in *is* or *are*:

1 The Millers _____ visiting their friends in Germany.

2 Mike _____ going to Spain.

3 Sophie _____ staying at a holiday flat in Exeter.

4 Julie and John _____ working in June.

Nun führe die Sätze fort. Ergänze den richtigen Satzanfang aus dem Kasten.

5 _____ going by car.

6 _____ going by train.

7 _____ going with her parents.

8 _____ going to Trinidad later.

→ • He's
• She's
• They're (2x)

2 **My weekend** Linda hat sich Notizen für eine E-Mail an ihren Cousin Nick gemacht.
Sie will ihm sagen, was sie am Wochenende vorhat, und sie will ihn fragen, was er plant.
Lies die Notizen und vervollständige die E-Mail. Benutze die *ing*-Form.

Saturday: have birthday party – friends come – go to swimming pool
Sunday: stay at home – help mum in garden – watch TV
Ask: do at weekend?

Tipp:
Vorsicht bei *have* und *come*:
Das „e" fällt vor „ing" weg.

Dear Nick,

On Saturday I'm (1) _____ a birthday party.

My friends are (2) _____ and we're (3) _____ to the swimming pool.

I think that's cool.

On Sunday I'm (4) _____ at home. I'm (5) _____ my mum in the garden. Then

I'm (6) _____ TV. It's Teen Pop on Sunday!

And what are you (7) _____ at the weekend? Is the weather nice in Spain?

Lots of love,

Linda

1 **Signs** Read the signs. Where can you find them?
Schreibe jeweils den richtigen Buchstaben in das Kästchen unten.

A	Don't leave litter here.

E	Buses and trams cannot stop fast.

B	*Please use headphones with your radio.*

F	**Welcome to Jim's party. This way for cake and cola. Say hi to the dog. Her name is Sally.**

C	Take your bag, money and camera with you.

G	**Holidays July 24th to September 4th. Have fun, pupils.**

D	**Quiet please! Other people want watch the film too.**

H	**For planes to Spain, please wait here.**

1 in a street ☐

2 at an airport ☐

3 in a classroom ☐

4 in a garden ☐

5 in a park ☐

6 on the beach ☐

7 in a car park ☐

8 at a cinema ☐

2 **A postcard** Finish the postcard with the missing small words.

> Tipp: Dein Schülerbuch kann dir dabei helfen. Schau auf S. 80.

Dear John,

I'm (1) _____ holiday (2) _____ my

children. We're (3) _____ a farm, Red Hill

Farm. Sue says (4) _____'s great. She says there are (5) _____

of things (6) _____ do here. (7) _____

afternoon she's feeding the animals. But Mike says it's boring.

He has (8) _____ plans. It's computer, computer, computer.

Wie fit bist du nun? Alles im grünen Bereich?
Mache den Check und male dabei die Ampeln entsprechend aus.

1 Vocabulary Put in the missing words.

1 Let's have a p_____c on the b_____h.

2 Let's buy o_____s from S_____n.

3 Let's go to Exeter s_____n and have a t_____p to Exmouth.

4 Let's watch *James Bond* at the c_____a

   this e_____g.

5 Let's i_____e Jim to our p_____y.

6 Let's go to the c_____e at Exmouth and have

   an i_____ cream.

Lösungen: Seite 68

0–2 richtige Antworten: rot

3–4 richtige Antworten: gelb

5–6 richtige Antworten: grün

2 Communication Circle the right words.

1 What are you *doing / going* at the weekend?

2 *When's / What's* your birthday?

3 *What / Who* are you inviting?

4 What are you doing *next / this* evening?

5 What *about / with* next Sunday?

6 I'm not *surprise / sure*.

Lösungen: Seite 68

0–2 richtige Antworten: rot

3–4 richtige Antworten: gelb

5–6 richtige Antworten: grün

3 Practice Bilde die richtige Form des Verbs in Klammern.

Example: (buy) Here's Harry. He ... a train ticket tomorrow.
→ Here's Harry. He's buying a train ticket tomorrow.

1 (go) He_____ to London next week.

2 (visit) He_____ his grandma.

3 (come) His sister Meg _____ with him.

4 (stay) They_____ at grandma's house.

5 (have) Grandma _____ a party. It's her birthday.

6 (buy) Harry and Meg _____ her a present tomorrow.

Lösungen: Seite 68

0–2 richtige Antworten: rot

3–4 richtige Antworten: gelb

5–6 richtige Antworten: grün

CHECK UNIT 5

4 **Reading** **Read the text.**

A postcard from a terrible holiday

Dear John,

This is a terrible holiday. We're in a house on a farm. The farm is so boring. The farm shop is terrible too. You can't get DVDs there. There are no other shops in the village. The animals are boring too. Red Hill Farm has cows – lots of them. No horses, no pigs, no sheep, no chickens. The holiday house is old and dirty and there's no TV. Dad likes it here! He sits in the garden and reads. My sister likes it too. We're coming home next weekend. Do you know what the name of the house is? It's Happy Holiday House – the wrong name, I say!

See you soon,

Mike

Circle **the right words.**

1 Mike says the farm is *great* / *boring*.

2 The farm shop *sells* / *doesn't sell* DVDs.

3 There are *cows* / *cows and other animals* on the farm.

4 The holiday house is *old* / *new*.

5 Dad *likes* / *doesn't like* the holiday.

6 Mike thinks the house has the *right* / *wrong* name.

Lösungen: Seite 68

0–2 richtige Antworten: rot

3–4 richtige Antworten: gelb

5–6 richtige Antworten: grün

5 **Writing** **Help Alex with his e-mail in English.**

Er will seinem E-Mail-Freund aus dem Urlaub schreiben, dass …

1 es toll ist hier auf dem Bauernhof: _____.

2 es hier ein nettes Mädchen gibt, Julia: _____.

3 es hier viele Sachen gibt, die man machen kann:

_____.

4 er heute Nachmittag die Tiere füttert: _____.

5 er morgen in ein Museum geht: _____.

6 Julia auch kommt: _____.

Lösungen: Seite 68

0–2 richtige Antworten: rot

3–4 richtige Antworten: gelb

5–6 richtige Antworten: grün

A NEW START

Test S.2

1 Vocabulary
1 pencil, <u>bag</u>, rubber, pen
2 OK, nice, great, <u>terrible</u>
3 you, I, we, <u>with</u>
4 look, listen, <u>sign</u>, see
5 hi, hello, <u>happy</u>, bye
6 <u>September</u>, Monday, Friday, Sunday

2 Communication
1 Good morning, Mr Jones.
  – Good morning, Tom.
2 Bye, Mum. – Bye, Pat.
3 Hi, Jane. – I'm not Jane. I'm Jill.
4 Hello. How are you? – I'm fine, thanks.
5 Hello, John. – Hello, Ms Black.
6 Hi. What's your name? – Hi. I'm Paul.

3 Practice
1 *I'm*
2 *He's*
3 *They're*
4 *I'm*
5 *aren't*
6 *aren't*

Test S.3

4 Reading
1 "boy"
2 nice
3 is
4 year 7
5 bag
6 Sammy

5 Writing
1 m
2 I'm
3 year
4 is
5 bag
6 time

Train *Vocabulary* S.4

1 What is it?
1 ein Bus
2 eine Tasche
3 ein Federmäppchen
4 ein Mädchen
5 ein Junge
6 eine Spinne

2 Colours
blau: Mrs Jones, mum, pupil
rot: pencil, sign, TV
grün: find, finish, repeat
orange: great, OK, right

3 Find the words
1 word
2 sentence
3 verse
4 story
5 Thanks.
6 Goodbye.
7 time
8 order
9 year
10 homework

S	D	U	D	B	A	L	T	I	M	E
T	S	T	O	R	Y	X	H	N	T	L
S	G	S	R	E	Y	E	A	R	D	S
C	O	I	D	N	A	L	N	H	Y	P
H	O	M	E	W	O	R	K	O	T	X
O	D	R	R	O	G	M	S	R	T	O
K	B	V	E	R	S	E	W	I	A	G
N	Y	V	M	D	D	Z	O	P	S	I
S	E	N	T	E	N	C	E	G	A	R
T	U	B	I	O	C	H	O	R	K	T

Train *Vocabulary* S.5

4 Which word is right?
1 school
2 teachers
3 pupils
4 pupil
5 bag
6 pencil case, books, pencils, pen

LÖSUNGEN

5 The missing letter
R I G H T

6 Questions
1 it
2 they
3 she
4 he
5 you
6 we

Train *Communication* S.6

1 What are they saying?
1 Bye
2 Hi
3 Good morning
4 tomorrow
5 Goodbye

2 Questions and answers
1 What's your name?
2 What year are you in?
3 How are you?
4 I'm Peter Williams.
5 I'm in year 7.
6 I'm fine, thanks.

3 What are they saying?
1 *I'm* German.
2 I'm *not* happy.
3 *I'm* fine, thank you.

4 Hi!
1 What's your name?
2 What's your name?
3 I'm
4 What
5 I'm

Train *Practice* S.7

1 Tim and Pam
1 *Tim isn't a girl. He's a* boy.
2 *Pam isn't a boy. She's a* girl.
3 *Tim and Pam aren't teachers They're* pupils.
4 *Pam: I'm not Tim. I'm* Pam.
5 *Tim: You aren't dangerous,* Pam. *You're* nice.

6 *Tim and Pam: Our school isn't in Exeter. It's in* London.
7 *Tim and Pam: We aren't German. We're* English.

2 No!
1 isn't
2 aren't
3 isn't
4 'm not
5 aren't
6 aren't
7 isn't

Train *Reading and writing* S.8

1 A poem
1 Troy
2 Sherman
3 Peacher
4 Gumm
5 Glad
6 Ryder

2 And you?
Lösungsbeispiel:
1 I'm *a* boy.
2 I'm Murat.
3 I'm *a* pupil.
4 I'm *in* year 5.
5 I'm happy.
6 I'm nice.

Check S.9

1 Vocabulary
1 great – terrible
2 Mr – Ms
3 mum – dad
4 pupil – teacher
5 hello – goodbye
6 please – thanks

2 Communication
1 morning
2 Peter
3 tomorrow
4 thanks
5 What's
6 year

3 Practice

1 She's
2 He's
3 They're
4 We're
5 You're
6 I'm

Check S.10

4 Reading

1 boy
2 He isn't
3 Port
4 7
5 He's
6 Jack

5 Writing

1 *I'm* a girl.
2 *I'm* Saskia.
3 *I'm* German
4 *I'm* a pupil.
5 *I'm* in year 5.
6 *It's* homework time.

UNIT 1

Test S.11

1 Vocabulary

1 home, house, <u>page</u>, flat
2 bed, chair, table, <u>garden</u>
3 mum, <u>room</u>, brother, sister
4 <u>group</u>, kitchen, living room, bedroom
5 <u>big</u>, brown, blue, red
6 old, dirty, wrong, <u>share</u>

2 Communication

1 Do you have a sister?
  – Yes, I do – Sally.
2 What colour is your room?
  – It's yellow and red.
3 Do you have your own room?
  – No, I don't. I share a room with Sally.
4 What's your name?
  – I'm Pat.
5 How old are you?
  – I'm 11.
6 What's in your room?
  – A big TV.

3 Practice

1 have
2 have
3 have
4 don't
5 doesn't
6 don't

Test S.12

4 Reading

	Yes.	No.
1		✔
2		✔
3		✔
4		✔
5	✔	
6	✔	

5 Writing

1 I have
2 I live
3 I'm in
4 I'm at
5 What colour
6 Do you have

Train *Vocabulary* S.13

1 My family

S	D	A	D	E	A	L	I	C	H
T	O	I	S	T	G	X	L	I	T
S	I	S	T	E	R	P	F	Y	D
C	H	I	S	W	A	L	K	H	Y
U	Z	T	R	A	N	F	W	O	T
S	G	R	A	N	D	M	A	R	T
K	F	U	P	L	A	S	T	N	A
N	M	U	M	B	D	Z	O	P	S
F	R	U	G	E	N	M	E	G	A
R	O	B	R	O	T	H	E	R	T

1	G	R	A	N	D	M	A
2	B	R	O	T	H	E	R
3	S	I	S	T	E	R	
4	M	U	M				
5	D	A	D				
6	G	R	A	N	D	A	D

= G E R M A N

LÖSUNGEN

2 Colours
PINK YELLOW RED WHITE BROWN
GREEN BLUE

Train *Vocabulary* S.14

3 Our house

1					B	E	D			
2				T	A	B	L	E		
3			K	I	T	C	H	E	N	
4				C	H	A	I	R		
5				G	A	R	D	E	N	
6		C	U	P	B	O	A	R	D	
7	L	I	V	I	N	G	R	O	O	M
8		B	E	D	R	O	O	M		

4 This is Jack.
1   live (L)
2   have (E)
3   share (S)
4   collect (L)
5   pick (P)
= S P E L L

Train *Communication* S.15

1 Do you have …?
1   Do you have your own room?
2   Do you have a TV in the room?
3   Do you have brothers and sisters?
4   Do you have a best friend?

2 Questions
1   What
2   How old are you
3   Where
4   Who

3 *Yes, I do or No, I don't?*
1   do
2   don't
3   Yes, I do
4   Yes, I do
5   I don't

4 Sammy
1   your name
2   old are you
3   Yes
4   Do you have a

5   Do you have *your own* room?
    – *No*, I don't.

Train *Practice* S.16

1 What do they have?
1   house, garden
2   bike, dog
3   grandma, grandad

2 Rosie and Tim
We have 7 bags, 12 pencils, 3 pens!
(= 22 things)

Train *Reading and writing* S.17

1 A poem
1   ~~Ja.~~ / Nein.
2   ~~Ja.~~ / Nein.
3   ~~Ja.~~ / Nein.
4   ~~Ja.~~ / Nein.
5   Haustiere. / ~~Alte Menschen~~.

2 And you?
Lösungsbeispiel:
1   *I'm* 10.
2   *I'm from* Bad Hainsee.
    I live in Orffstraße.
3   I'm at Erich-Kästner-*Schule*.
    I'm in *year 5*.
4   I don't have *my own room*.
5   I don't have *a sister*.
6   I have two *brothers*.

Check S.18

1 Vocabulary
1   table – chair
2   kitchen – bathroom
3   brother – sister
4   nice – terrible
5   house – flat
6   old – new

2 Communication
1   Do you have a spider?
2   What's your name?
3   What colour is your spider?
4   Do you have lots of friends?
5   Do you have a cupboard in your room?
6   Do you have grandmas and grandads?

3 Practice
1 has
2 doesn't have
3 have
4 don't have
5 have
6 has

Check S. 19
4 Reading
1 house
2 big
3 kitchen
4 bathroom
5 nice
6 family

5 Writing
1 *I* have a brother and a sister.
2 *I* live in Konstanz.
3 *I'm* at Schillerschule.
4 *I* don't have my own room.
5 *I* don't have a pet.
6 *My* brother has a spider.

UNIT 2

Test S. 20
1 Vocabulary
1 *chickens*, pigs, sheep
2 *cats*, dogs, hamsters
3 *village*, country, farm
4 *mother*, father, grandad
5 *get up*, come, go
6 *every day*, at eight o'clock, usually

2 Communication
1 I get up at eight o'clock.
2 I play a game with dad.
3 I have breakfast at half past eight.
4 What do you do on Sundays?
5 I ride my quad.
6 When do you go home?

3 Practice
1 go
2 comes
3 work

4 helps
5 come
6 watches

Test S. 21
4 Reading
1 Yes. ☐ No. ✔
2 Yes. ✔ No. ☐
3 Yes. ✔ No. ☐
4 Yes. ☐ No. ✔
5 Yes. ☐ No. ✔
6 Yes. ☐ No. ✔

5 Writing
1 *I* get up *at half past* seven.
2 *I* have breakfast at eight o'clock.
3 *I* go to school at half past eight.
4 *I* come home at half past four.
5 *I* watch TV at seven o'clock.
6 *I* go to bed at nine o'clock.

Train *Vocabulary* S. 22
1 Animals
sheep, fish, dog = pig
bird, cat, hamster = rat
chicken, horse = cow

2 Find the words

```
H E R H I P L O U Y T R I N G
L S E Y B R O C H I C K E N S
G F F I S H V O T M N X I S T
Z S P R T I D U M O R L P E V
I D I C T I O N A R I E S C I
O C H A N Y R T G U D F T O L
A W E E C H O R S E S B O H L
T C O W S A D I K L H U R N A
C G R O U S A E W H E L I N G
F A M I L I E S B U E T E Y E
N E D F P O L R T A P S S D S
```

1 chickens, horses, cows, villages
2 dictionaries, families, countries, stories
3 fish, sheep

LÖSUNGEN

Train *Vocabulary* S. 23

3 My school days
1 get
2 have
3 go
4 come
5 do
6 play
7 watch
8 go

4 When and where?
Zeit: every day, half past six, usually, after school, at eight o'clock
Ort: at the window, to the shop, in the country, near Kenn, on the farm

Train *Communication* S. 24

1 On Saturdays
1 I get up at ten o'clock.
2 I have breakfast at half past ten.
3 I play with my friends.
4 I go to a big shop.
5 I watch TV.

2 Questions
1 When do you get up?
2 When do you go to school?
3 When do you come home?
4 What do you do on Saturdays?
5 What do you do on Sundays?

3 What's right?
1 get up
2 Saturdays
3 have breakfast
4 ride my quad bike
5 half past four
6 friends

4 A dialogue
1 What do you do
2 When do you
3 What do you do
4 do after, I watch
5 do after, I go
6 I go

Train *Practice* S. 25

1 Who?
1 Kevin
2 The Browns
3 Grandma
4 Mum

2 Every Sunday ...
1 get
2 ride
3 plays
4 comes
5 watches, read
6 go

Train *Reading and writing* S. 26

1 Who am I?
1 Tess
2 Jamie
3 Mr Fraser
4 Sarah
5 Mrs Fraser

2 Pat
1 at seven o'clock
2 have breakfast
3 at eight o'clock
4 at four o'clock
5 play a game
6 go to bed, nine o'clock

Check S. 27

1 Vocabulary
1 chickens, pigs, dogs, cows
2 cats, dogs, sheep, hamsters
3 wheelchair, car, bus, animal
4 watch, get up, come, go
5 on Saturdays, usually, play, every day
6 country, town, farm, breakfast

2 Communication
1 I do my homework.
2 I ride my quad bike.
3 I play with Sammy.
4 I play games with my friends.
5 I help at home.
6 I get up at 7 o'clock.

3 Practice

1 go
2 works
3 helps
4 goes
5 waits
6 go

Check S. 28

4 Reading

1 lives
2 He's
3 Tess
4 works
5 afternoon
6 Jamie

5 Writing

1 *I* get up at seven o'clock.
2 *I* go to school at half past eight.
3 *I* play football.
4 *I* watch TV with my brother.
5 *I* usually watch "Eurostars".
6 *I* go to bed at nine o'clock.

UNIT 3

Test S. 29

1 Vocabulary

1 swimming *pool*
2 *month*
3 pet *shop*
4 go *dancing*
5 *her*
6 *class*

2 Communication

1 I like dogs. They're great
2 I like football. It's a good sport.
3 I like "Eurostars". It's great.
4 I don't like cats. They're boring.
5 I don't like tennis. It's a terrible sport.
6 I don't like school. It's a terrible place.

3 Practice

1 doesn't
2 don't
3 doesn't
4 don't
5 doesn't
6 doesn't

Test S. 30

4 Reading

1 Right. ✔   Wrong. ☐
2 Right. ✔   Wrong. ☐
3 Right. ☐   Wrong. ✔
4 Right. ☐   Wrong. ✔
5 Right. ✔   Wrong. ☐
6 Right. ☐   Wrong. ✔

5 Writing

1 I like *football*.
2 I like dogs.
3 I like magazines.
4 I don't *like* music.
5 I don't like tennis.
6 I don't like cats.

Train *Vocabulary* S. 31

1 Crossword

					S	P	O	R	T	Y	
							O	F			
			B	A	L	L	E	T			
M	U				E	E					
U	Y				E	E			E		
S			E	X	P	E	N	S	I	V	E
I	D	E	A						E		
C		S		P	R	E	S	E	N	T	
T	O	Y		A		P	I				
				R		Y	O	U	N	G	
W	A	L	K			R	G				
				E	A	T					

LÖSUNGEN

2 **The right word**
1 her
2 you
3 him
4 me
= home

Train *Vocabulary* S.32

3 **Partners**
1 clothes shop
2 youth club
3 pet shop
4 fish and chip shop
5 sports shop
6 bookshop
7 supermarket
8 swimming pool
9 CD shop

4 **I can't!**
1 buy
2 eat
3 sleep
4 think
5 walk
6 feed
= QUESTIONNAIRE

Train *Communication* S.33

1 **Tina**
1 don't like
2 like
3 like
4 don't like

2 **... and Bob**
1 I don't like football. It's dangerous.
2 I don't like pets. They're lots of work.
3 I don't like "Teen Music Scene".
   It's terrible.

3 **Pete and Paul**
1 *I don't* buy CDs.
2 *I don't* watch "Teen Music Scene".
3 I don't like football.
4 I don't eat hamburgers.

4 **New friends**
1 I don't like
2 What about you?

3 I don't like dogs.
4 like
5 sports magazines
6 watch "Teen Music Scene"

Train *Practice* S.34

1 **That isn't right! But what *is* right?**
1 Sharon doesn't have a cat.
   She has a dog.
2 The Millers don't live in Exeter.
   They live in London.
3 I don't play football. I play tennis.
4 My brother doesn't buy sports
   magazines. He buys music magazines.
5 We don't go dancing.
   We go swimming.
6 You don't get up late on Sundays.
   You get up early.
= SPORTY

2 **People**
1 Aysha likes music and basketball.
   She doesn't like cats, dogs, reading and
   volleyball.
2 Kevin likes dogs, music and volleyball.
   He doesn't like cats, reading and
   basketball.
3 Ben and Tim like cats, reading and
   basketball.
   They don't like dogs, music and
   volleyball.

Train *Reading and writing* S.35

1 **A questionnaire**
1 doesn't bite
2 eats
3 doesn't take
4 doesn't walk
5 doesn't come
6 likes

2 **And Meg?**
1 *I read* magazines.
2 *I don't* read books.
3 *I* play football.
4 *I* don't play tennis.
5 *I* don't buy CDs.
6 *I* buy magazines.

LÖSUNGEN

Check S.36

1 Vocabulary
1 bookshop, pet shop, supermarket
2 park, sports centre, swimming pool
3 nice, sporty, young
4 month, week, year
5 listen, talk, think
6 her, him, me

2 Communication
1 *I don't watch TV. It's boring.*
2 *I don't play football. It's terrible.*
3 *I don't buy CDs. They're expensive.*
4 *I don't like dogs. They're dangerous.*
5 *I don't like hamsters. They're dirty.*
6 *I don't read comics. They're boring.*

3 Practice
1 doesn't
2 don't
3 doesn't buy me magazines
4 don't have my own room
5 don't live in a big house
6 don't live near me

Check S.37

4 Reading

	Right.	Wrong.	Not in the text.
1	✔		
2			✔
3		✔	
4		✔	
5	✔		
6			✔

5 Writing
1 *I like dogs.*
2 *I don't like cats.*
3 *I buy lots of magazines.*
4 *I don't buy CDs.*
5 *I play tennis.*
6 *I don't play football.*

UNIT 4

Test S.38

1 Vocabulary
1 car – car park
2 money – bank
3 plane – airport
4 canoe – river
5 farmer – farm
6 light – bike

2 Communication
1 Do you often ride your bike?
2 Do your sisters like football?
3 Does your mum watch quiz shows on TV?
4 Do you have a favourite football team?
5 Do you want to play a game?
6 Does your brother live at home?

3 Practice
1 Does
2 Do
3 Does
4 Do
5 Does
6 Do

Test S.39

4 Reading
1 rides
2 bike
3 trainer
4 hand
5 right
6 answers

5 Writing
1 doesn't, signals
2 doesn't, tracks
3 on the
4 doesn't, lights
5 doesn't, at
6 lesson

Train *Vocabulary* S.40

1 Odd word out
1. stop, forget, shouted, <u>our</u>
2. better, modern, <u>farm</u>, electronic
3. parents, <u>very</u>, driver, farmer
4. tram, money, <u>modern</u>, motorbike
   "Our farm *is* very modern!"

2 What? Where?
1. *p*lanes, *a*irport
2. *c*ars, *c*ar park
3. *b*ikes, *b*ike track
4. *m*otorbikes, *r*oad
5. *m*ountain bike
6. *on* foot, *p*avement

Train *Vocabulary* S.41

3 Partners
black – track; bring – spring; light – write;
line – sign; plane – train; sport – thought

4 Football fans
1. went
2. wanted
3. were
4. were
5. shouted
6. thought
7. went
8. saw

						¹S	A	²W
³W	E	R	E			H		E
A						O		N
N						U		T
⁴T	H	O	U	G	H	T		
E						E		
D						D		

Train *Communication* S.42

1 Bob and his questions
1. Do you go to the swimming pool?
2. Do you want to play football?
3. Do you want to listen to my new CD?
4. Do you like cats and dogs?

2 Matt and his answers
2. No, I don't. I don't like football.
3. Yes, I do. I like *The Huggers*.
4. Yes, I do. They're great pets.

3 More questions
1. Does your dad like his job?
2. Does your mum often see her friends?
3. Does your brother live in a new flat?
4. Do your friends come to your house?
5. Do your mum and dad buy magazines
   for you?
6. Does your dog play with cats?

4 Terrible Terry
1. she does
2. Does your, work
3. No, he doesn't.
4. your mum
5. Do
6. Does she
7. Does she help

Train *Practice* S.43

1 Questions with *Yes/No* answers
1. Do you get to school on foot?
   – Yes, I do.
2. Does your brother like motorbikes?
   – No, he doesn't.
3. Does your sister always use bike tracks?
   – Yes, she does.
4. Do your parents often go to work
   by train? – No, they don't.
5. Does your bike have lights?
   – Yes, it does.
6. Do we have to do our homework?
   – Yes, we do.
= DRIVER

LÖSUNGEN

2 Who likes what?

1 Do you like your dog?
2 Does Tim like his room?
3 Do the pupils like their teacher?
4 Does Ms Brown like her class?
5 Does Mr Fraser like his farm?
6 Does Pam like her brother?
7 Do the Millers like their car?

Train *Reading and writing* S. 44

1 Jobs

1	teacher	E
2	farmer	G
3	bus driver	D
4	baggage handler	C
5	a job in a tourist information	A
6	a job in a band	H
7	road safety trainer	F
8	a job in a bank	B

2 Questions

1 Do your friends always do their homework?
2 Does your sister buy her clothes in Exeter?
3 Are you often in the park with your friends?
4 Is your dad happy with his job?
5 Can you come with us, please?
6 Am I your best friend?

Check S. 45

1 Vocabulary

1 train
2 electronic
3 baggage handler
4 his
5 wanted
6 street

2 Communication

1 *Does*
2 *Do* your brothers live at home?
3 *Does* your mum work at the bank?
4 *Do* your friends watch TV?
5 *Do* you like Chelsea?
6 *Do* our teachers live near the school?

3 Practice

1 Do
2 Does
3 Do
4 Does
5 Do
6 Does

Check S. 46

4 Reading

1 Pepper is Tom Price's ~~dog~~. cat
2 Pepper often goes to the ~~shops~~. airport
3 Mr Price ~~knows~~ this. doesn't know
4 Pepper goes in the ~~trains~~. planes
5 He ~~often~~ comes home in the evening. always
6 Pepper says there's no place like ~~school~~. home

5 Writing

1 Do you like football?
2 Do you often watch TV?
3 Do you have a pet?
4 Does your mum have a job?
5 Does your brother live at home?
6 Do you write lots of e-mails?

UNIT 5

Test S. 47

1 Vocabulary

1 beach
2 orange
3 August
4 evening
5 milk
6 ice cream

2 Communication

1 When's your birthday? – It's in July.
2 What are you doing on your birthday? – I'm having a party.
3 Who are you inviting? – Paul, Tim, all my friends.
4 What are you doing this evening? – I'm helping mum this evening.
5 What are you doing next Saturday? – Next Saturday? I'm not sure.
6 Do you want to come to Jamie's farm? – Yes, please – great!

3 Practice

1 'm staying
2 is staying
3 is having
4 're going
5 are visiting
6 're going

Test S.48

4 Reading

1 week
2 big
3 in Jim's garden
4 play football
5 is
6 don't know

5 Writing

1 We're going to Spain for two weeks.
2 I'm not going on holiday this year.
3 I'm staying at home in the holidays.
4 I'm visiting my grandma and old friends.
5 It's my birthday in July.
6 I'm having a big party at 7 o'clock.

Train *Vocabulary* S.49

1 The third word

1 banana
2 August
3 milk
4 sea
5 Spain
6 museum
7 chocolate
= CHAIRPERSON

2 What is it?

1 museum
2 Spain
3 cinema
4 station
5 cafe
6 beach

Train *Vocabulary* S.50

3 What are the questions?

1 get, tea
2 have, party
3 stay, holiday flat
4 go, holiday
5 invite, friends
6 visit, dad

4 Crossword

	S	O	O	N			O	T	H	E	R	
	R							R				
A		A		P	I	C	N	I	C		F	
P	L	A	N	O				P			U	
P		G		S		S			S	U	N	
L		W	E	A	T	H	E	R	U			
E				C		A			M	A	Y	
				A					M			
		S	U	R	P	R	I	S	E			
				D					R			

Train *Communication* S.51

1 Birthdays

1 August
2 Pat – It's in July.
3 Dave – It's in January.
4 Tim – It's in March.
5 Sally – It's in June.

2 What are their plans?

1 I'm going to town with mum.
2 I'm helping dad in the kitchen.
3 I'm playing football with Tom.
4 I'm having a big party next week.
5 I'm inviting my friends to the party.

3 Questions

1 When's your birthday?
2 What are you doing on Saturday?
3 Who are you inviting to your party?
4 Where are you going next weekend?
5 Do you want to come to town with me?

LÖSUNGEN

4 Terrible

1 are you doing
2 want to watch
3 What are you, next
4 I'm going
5 what
6 I'm having

Train *Practice* S.52

1 This summer …

1 are
2 is
3 is
4 are
5 They're
6 He's
7 She's
8 They're

2 My weekend

1 having
2 coming
3 going
4 staying
5 helping
6 watching
7 doing

Train *Reading and writing* S.53

1 Signs

1 E
2 H
3 G
4 F
5 B
6 A
7 C
8 D

2 A postcard

1 on
2 with
3 on
4 it
5 lots
6 to
7 In the
8 no

Check S.54

1 Vocabulary

1 *picnic*, *beach*
2 *oranges*, *Spain*
3 *station*, *trip*
4 *cinema*, *evening*
5 *invite*, *party*
6 *cafe*, *ice cream*

2 Communication

1 doing
2 When's
3 Who
4 this
5 about
6 sure

3 Practice

1 's going
2 's visiting
3 is coming
4 're staying
5 is having
6 are buying

Check S.55

4 Reading

1 boring
2 doesn't sell
3 cows
4 old
5 likes
6 wrong

5 Writing

1 It's great here on the farm.
2 There's a nice girl here, Julia.
3 There are lots of things to do here.
4 This afternoon I'm feeding the animals.
5 Tomorrow I'm going to a museum.
6 Julia is coming too.